A Coney Island State of Mind

For more information please contact ggaiamex@gmail.com
ISBN 9781079286717

A Coney Island State of Mind

POEMS, ILLUSTRATIONS & ILLUSTRATED POEMS 1990–2019

Gaia Schilke

To my places:

Falls Brook Farm in Connecticut;
Maine; Martha's Vineyard; Rhode Island; Costa
Rica; San Miguel de Allende, Mexico and, for the
defining experience of my life, New York City
(including Coney Island).

And to my people:

My mother Mim Nichols; my sisters Donna Schilke
& Joyce Cohen; my grandmother Josephine Waters;
my grandfather J. George Schilke; my dearest
nieces & nephews; my childhood
best friends Martha & Ellie;
and my beloved partner Collier Kear.

La gratitud a todos, por siempre y para siempre.

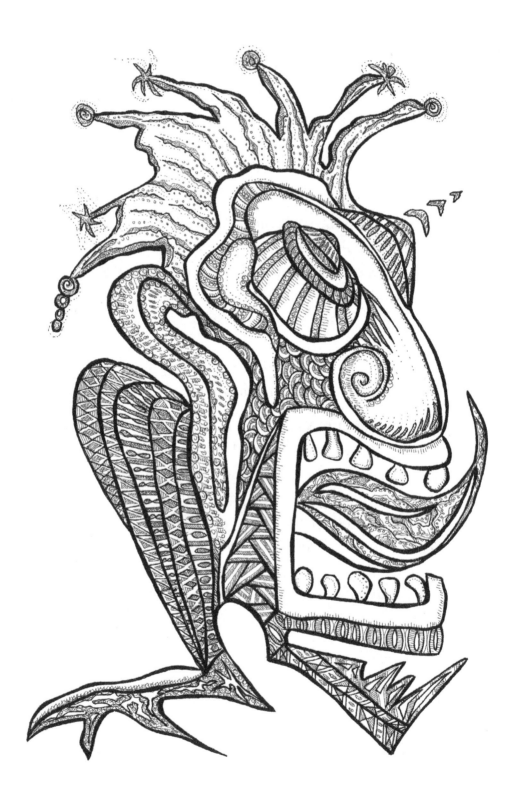

Contents

Part I: Poetry

White Castle 11

Legacy 13

Face of Old Glory 15

To the Boys 17

Henry Coney Island Miller 20

Las Bravas 24

Drinking from the Weirdwoman's Glass 26

Nocterminal .28

You Can't Eat While You're Blowing a Whistle 30

Listen You Man 32

I Am Not a Ghost, You Are Not the Wind* 34

From the Margin 36

Fuck Me: A Meditation 38

Don't Tell 42

The Malady of Death Meets the State of Desire 44

Mitzi Mitten Who Came Into My Life and Shined 48

I Tell You I Just Don't 51

Close But No Cigar 53

Ricky D 55

She Who Brings the Nectar 57

Diego and Frida 58

La Gratitud [for Collier] 59

When Color Becomes Suspect 64

Requiem 70

Grounds 75

Part II: Illustrated Poems

Henry Coney Island Miller 81

Nocterminal 85

Mitzi Mitten Who Came Into My Life and Shined 95

After .99

Listen You Man 108

Face of Old Glory 112

When Color Becomes Suspect 115

About the Author 127

Part I: Poetry

White Castle

Okay so it's 1:00 am
And you're driving and not riding through Brooklyn
And you know how Brooklyn
Goes on forever
And the further you go
The hungrier you get?

Plus you're driving and not riding
And they got White Castle out here
And you're a bunch of overgrown teenagers
Cruising and losing your high

I mean you want to move into
White Castle
But you're driving and not riding
And you're all too lazy to get out of the car

So you drive through the Drive-through
Only the Drive-through
Is running in place

And you end up doing time on that White Castle line
And it's like the people in front of you
Just left the car and walked home to eat

And Carl says, what did they order
The family reunion pack?
And Willie says, they call this fast food
'cause what you do is fast
And you're screaming at the car behind you
To Back Off, the end is not near

But then you're nosing up the window
And praise the Lords of Flatbush
White Castle delivers
99 cents for two burger wannabe's
And one defeated order of fries

And everyone shuts up now
Stuffing those wisecracks and feeling those burgers
Burn all the way down

And now you're ready to keep driving
Maybe even off the Brooklyn Bridge
With that fire in your gut

Legacy

The first time my grandfather saw my grandmother
He said, so the story goes
See that lady? I'm going to marry her
He knew right away about the pretty veneer
He did not know about the madness it contained
The package, you see, so lovely

I remember her as a wraith
Of isolation, religion and beauty
Restrained in a cold, sad home
Three times as a young mother she was hospitalized
Put away in an institute for the insane
In her eighties she confided to me
Those were the happiest times of her life
No children, no husband, no crowds
To serve but never sit down with

Just miles of solitude
A quiet, white pure space
To fill at leisure with words and music

Sometimes I feel that part of me
That is this grandmother
Longing to be put away
I cover my chest and turn
Look over my shoulder in fear
That there is a man looking at me
And clearing his throat to say
See that lady?

Face of Old Glory

Why not eat yourself you asked
And opening your mouth wide
You start with your feet
Salty sweaty dirty feet
Calloused and bent and tough

And you consume the beast
Wholly your own
Until you are up to your neck
In your mouth

And smiling a greedy smile
With fiery mane surrounding
Eyes luminous and bulgy

You chomp and gnaw and spit
Out the remains
Belch and lay backward

You close you eyes and dream
Of the next meal
Of juicy lips and scaly tongue

And the diners at your table
Raise their glasses
To salute you

To the Boys

To the boys I just met
To the boys I haven't yet met
To the boys I used to meet
To the boys, the boys, the boys
What is it about you boys anyhow?

I want you to come and sit on my lap
I want to whisper in your ears
All of them
I want to hold you, hold me
I want to know you, show me

I want to have your protection
Your umbrella please
I want you to open my doors
All of them

I want you to go away

I want you to come back again sometimes
I want you to excite me with your words
So I don't sleep at night
And I'm lying awake saying to myself:
First I said then he said then we said

And our voices fit together
Like Siamese twins
Only with room to breathe
And no fear of death

I want you boys
I want you to be better

So you boys you beautiful boys
I want you all
Or at least some of you
Or at least one of you
All right
Maybe half of one of you
But at least that

Listen you boys

Listen you boys
I know you're looking at me
I know what you see

But I'm showing you who you see
All you boys
Or one of you boys

I'm looking for you
With my heart in a sling

Henry Coney Island Miller

In December I go out to Coney Island to see a play adapted from Henry Miller's novel Black Spring. And Henry's there all right, and after the play's over he and I go down to Nathan's, grab us a couple of dogs, and head back up the boardwalk to watch the sun set on a cold Sunday afternoon. And I say to him, 'Henry, your play at Coney Island, it's an inspiration.' And Henry smiles that conspiring smile of his as he leans towards me, his eyes like gleaming picks. 'Baby', he says, 'Coney Island is my middle name.'

This poem includes words from Henry Miller's Black Spring.

* * *

At the sideshow by the seashore
With mirrors and magic tricks
And the slick under belly
Crooks its juicy finger

You want to eat fried things
You want to fight major spasms
In your gut
You want to move into
A hiding place for freaks

Henry Miller is not hiding

He wants to declare he is a traitor

Among traitors to the human race

And we look but we cannot bear it

Us whores and faggots and niggers

And cunts and kikes

We are all of us equal

In the waste and cruelty of our lives

I go with Henry

To his street of early sorrows

Where everything is shoddy

Thin as Pasteboard

A Coney Island of the mind

We all come here, finally

And we live in those buildings

That cannot hold themselves erect

Henry asks: What is all this

That I never forgot

And now is no more?

He says: I was a lamb

They cut away everything that was mine

All that was sacred, private, taboo

And now the war is inside me

My broken rectum howls

He is the bruised red son
Going down on Coney Island

Henry Miller beats off
Into the bloody and wild night life

When this mad thing called sleep
Runs like an eight-day clock
All pain and dull and bearable
Like this

Las Bravas

I wouldn't bet on it
I mean I could walk from here
To tomorrow and nothing
Would be any different

I spent days pitching my tent
In your front yard
Only to get invited indoors
Where the servants live

Look, I skate all over this city
I hit taxicabs with my fist
Kiss my middle finger
Shove it up their face

Maybe I can't find my way home anymore
But it's better than sleeping
With your eyes open
Guessing what everyone has to say
Before they lay flat their mouths

Listen, I know how to make pretty
You boys are easier than you think
But I don't want it that way

I want to shove it in your face
Wake you up then get you lost
I want to part you like a river
And spread my words
Inside of you

Drinking from
the Weirdwoman's Glass

The weirdwoman waits
And never gives up
Asks herself questions
She never answers
Wears black lace gloves
To tie back her hair

She hops on one foot
Knocks stars out of her ears

The weirdwoman drops
Crumbs of bread along her path
Birds pick them up
Fly them away
So no one can follow

The weirdwoman opens
Her arms then her legs
Then her heart
Revealing the same place
Soft and yearning

The weirdwoman floats
On still water
Marks the place her heart sank
Then rose to the surface

The weirdwoman laughs
Alone to herself
An echo without reply

A stranger's blessing

Nocterminal

Look, something told me I should
Just stay in tonight but no
I don't pay any attention to myself
I head out on my blades
Like a lamb to slaughter

And sure enough
As soon as I start my laps
Around Washington Square
This boy this adolescent type
Shimmies up on his bike
And tries to run me off the road

So I grab his bike and I won't let go
And now he knows it's him and me
We go down together or not at all

And he's scared and I'm glad
And I won't let go
But when I do I give him a shove
And he takes a dive

And I call him the expletive deleted he is
And his friend says
You hear what she called you?
And they both start after me

So I cross the park shaking bad
Decide to skip the skate altogether
Head for home with a vengeance
Deadbolt the door behind me

And look down from my window
At the smooth dark street below

You Can't Eat While You're Blowing a Whistle

Her father's words get stuck
In her throat like chicken bones
He washes them down
With another drink
Spits scarlet letters
In her alphabet soup

She spoons them around
Lets them grow cold
Swallows it whole

She sits alone in the kitchen
She says: This is how you make
Tomato soup fast
Slit your wrists and cry

She sees his face on her fist
Lowers it down to the bowl
Watches him drown
In the blood red soup

Listen You Man

Listen you man with two first names
Who do you think you are anyhow?
Coming into my life with your big spoon
And stirring up the elements

Bringing up hope from the bottom of the stew
Making the stew taste like caviar

Well never mind you man
I don't like, never have, never will caviar
And I don't eat that shit

But I will for you
Sorry that just slipped out

Look here you man you
Leave me alone
I want my hope back where it belongs
And I'm not dining at this table
Can I borrow your spoon?

You southern sweetbread
You man with two names
As if a man with one name
Weren't already one too many

So don't offer me this
Did you offer by the way?
I want to forget you
I want to memorize you

I want to stop wanting
You know I just want to stop wanting

Please stop stirring me
Just long enough to
Listen

I Am Not a Ghost, You Are Not the Wind*

It is so easy to slip away
And I tell you there is no hope
For any of us
If we choose not to see this

So easy to slip away
Into the drowning pool below
Drop-kicked from a sinking ship
Women and children first

I am not a ghost
You may walk around me
You may look right through me
But when you do not see me
You let me slip away

You are not the wind
I will not be moved
I will be in your face

Until you begin to see me
In your mirror it is so easy

It is so easy
To slip away

Called out to passing crowd by a homeless man in NYC

From the Margin

The BBC asks Jean Genet
About l'amour
L'amour? Genet laughs
I thought you said la mort

No, l'amour, BBC insists
What about l'amour in prison
Was there one special boy?

Not one, Genet rolls his eyes
Hundreds

And Genet indicts the family
As the first criminal cell
He mourns the children
With all their struggles
All their humiliations
All their courage

But one must pay says Genet
For the pleasures of stealing
And the robbed child returns
To every cell in all the prisons

One special boy

A hundred special boys

And more

L'amour

La mort

Fuck Me: A Meditation

You know when you stop
And stare out your window
Looking for something to inspire
To take you higher
To light your fire

And all you're getting
Are lines from 60s songs?

You know the times you contemplate
Window gates and fire escapes
Cloud shades drawn down
Over empty rooms

But then you see it, there
Written in dust on a window
With a finger inside
A call to us on the outside

Fuck Me it says
And even though workmen come and go
No one has removed this message

Not Fuck You but Fuck Me it says
And it starts me thinking

I had a friend who whenever
She messed up would groan
Slap her head and say, 'Fuuuuuuuk me!'

On the street there's the warning
Don't try to fuck me, man

Then there's your basic begging fuck me
You know the plea
The one that comes
With fingers pulling hair
You know the one
That's music to your ears

I look up Fuck Me in Webster's Dictionary
And there it isn't
Between fuchsia and fuddle

Right there where it does not belong
Not Fuck Me or even Fuck
Although the word after fuddle
Is fuddy-duddy

So there it still is

Fuck Me as a message to the world

Or at least East 6th Street

Between A & B

Or the southern half

Of this one city block

Or maybe it was written

Especially for me

To wake up every day

Until I saw it

As a poem

Tomorrow I might turn

Look the other way

And it will be gone

Fuck Me! It shouts

Traveling down the street

Fuck Me! It screams

Looking for a song

41

Don't Tell

When Grandma said good-bye that winter
I knew she wasn't coming back
That my ally had defected forever
She didn't know but I did

When I answered the phone that night
My parents were entertaining friends
Laughing drinking flirting
Ready to go out to dinner

My uncle was calling with bad news
Grandma was dying she was dying
And she was never coming back

The laughing drinking flirting spinning room
And me clutching the phone
Dad took the phone and he took the bad news
And he told me not to tell

Don't tell Mom that her mother is dying
Don't tell Mom that Grandma is dying
Don't tell stop crying keep quiet

Stop

Because we're ready to go out now
We want to keep laughing drinking
Not knowing

I stopped kept quiet didn't tell Mom
She didn't know but I did

The Malady of Death
Meets the State of Desire

His eyes traveled up inside her that night
Painful eyes, festering eyes from far away
Later, up close, she saw they were the eyes
Of a child who had been kicked around a lot
And deep down where she was good at seeing
She caught a glimmer of sweetness
And he saw her see it

He held her eyes then, even caressed them gently
And she flashed her desiring eyes all over him
Up and down, until he felt his sex reach out
Beyond his own grasp, and that made him bend
And smell her hair

Then she leaned into him light but with skin prickly
Through all the layers
Of city winter black and blue

He led her home and she followed
Real close but skeptical

And they fell in love that night, love
Like a ladder propped up against a house
On fire, when for just a few seconds
The ladder is the safest place to be

And for a few moments they reflect the danger
And the passion
And death doesn't matter then
See, this is the point

But the next day he is far away
He wants to rip out the part
Made soft by his longing
Traveling up and down
From eyes to breasts
From head to sex

And he wonders how to escape
This weakened state, see
He never wanted to go on living
And never in the state of desire

She holds herself, whispers softly in his ear
She thinks she has never seen
Such tender eyes before

She knows how it is to see too much too soon
She knows how it is to lose hope
And she sees how it will be
With all the loving and leaving and coming
And gone

But she knows how to do this
To circle his skin with licks of wet warmth
Finding one more reason for one more day

And the pain after, a solid shut window
Up against a brick wall
Pain that curls her in a ball
And holds her breath

Even that gives her a reason

See, she lives in the state of desire
Where death beckons

But it cannot contain

Mitzi Mitten
Who Came Into My Life
and Shined

She had long, long legs, Mitzi Mitten
And short white hair
She was the closest thing
To a real live Barbie doll
I had ever seen
I was seven, and in love

She came to visit
But instead of her husband Bob
She brought her lover Bill
We didn't care, we the whole family
Were in love, and she could do anything
She wanted and we'd hold open her doors
Sweep her path and carry her bags

She didn't have any of her own kids, Mitzi Mitten
But she did have Snoop and Smooch
Her two stuffed dog children
Who traveled with her every where
And were all dressed up with watches
That ticked suspiciously like our own

She confided to me that they both drank
Too much vodka, and that Snoop
Had his eye on me when Smooch wasn't looking
But then they were pretty advanced for their age

She and her lover Bill took us girls
To Honey Island
From there we could see the islands
Called Three Sisters, like us
We fished and rocked in the hammock
And brought shells to lay at the feet of Mitzi Mitten
The feet at the end of those long, long legs

She explained to us girls the real deal
About cosmetic application
And the exact right way to apply perfume
Which is not, by the way
To dab it on your skin
But to spray the air
In front of you and waltz
Through the mist just so

When Mitzi Mitten came to school with Snoop

My big sister was red-faced, but not me

I know all the kids were wondering

How I got to be so lucky

As to know a real live movie star

She told my teacher she was thinking about

Enrolling Snoop in my school

And could she ask come questions please?

My teacher looked at me with raised eyebrows

But I didn't care

I was in love and learning

Important things about what it meant

To be a grown up woman

With a mind of her own

I Tell You I Just Don't

The truth about this is
There is no truth about this
Depends which way you bend
Depends which way you take it

Maybe I don't care if you care if I care
Maybe I conjure your image there and there
Then again, maybe I don't

It might have been just a week ago
Fingers touched a slight blow
Eyes marched over the bridge to hearts
And I said I don't care

And you were there
Waiting, by a shallow pool below
I said I don't care
And plunged towards your shadow

I told you about the ward at Bellevue
For people who think they are Jesus Christ
You told me about the ward in Macon, Georgia
For people who think they're
The Hoochie-Coochie Man

And I said I don't care
Where I've been before
And I said I don't care
Where you're going next

And we danced a timid two-step
A bump and grind behind
A sea of Calla lilies

Knowing they would die soon
I said I just don't care
I said just to see them in bloom
You said just to see them uprooted

And I still feel you deep inside me
Now I tell you I just don't care

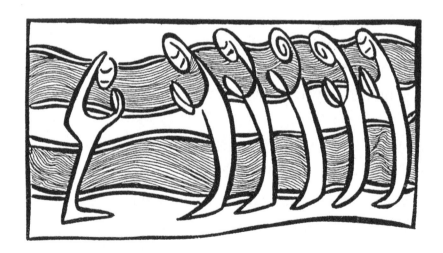

Close But No Cigar

I almost fucked the cab driver
Last night I came close
To taking him home
Or just taking him
There in the cab

He picked me up
He thought I would
Saw the slippery line
Between desire
And my foot out the door

He told me no charge
He picked me up
The stirring thing
Filled the cab
He told me no charge
He thought I would
And I almost did

My foot out the door

I took it upstairs
The stirring thing
That nasty tender
Juicy thing

I brought it home
I put it here
I'm fucking you

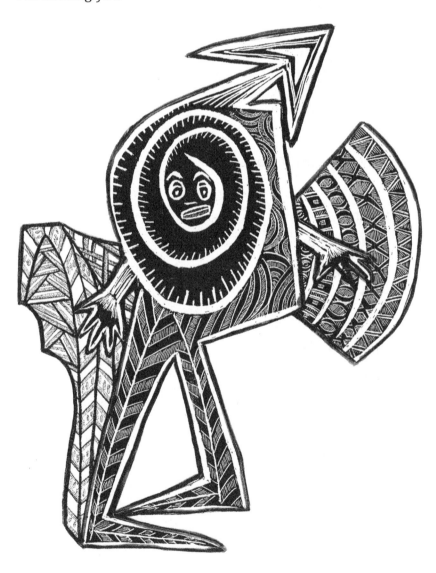

Ricky D

Let's get small Ricky D
In the front seat times two
This boy never gets high
Straight as a pin
And twice as sharp
And he's got laughs to go
High or no

Let's get small Ricky D
Watch the nether world
Out the rear view, you
Broadcasting the scenario
And singing like Prince
How he'd drink every ounce

And now I see why
No need for the high
When you're whack to begin with

Ricky D's on a roll
And the car's running too
He sings in my ear
If I was your girlfriend

And we got laughs
We got laughs to go
Ricky D's on a roll
And I'm running too

I sing in his ear
Ricky D
Let's Go

She Who Brings the Nectar

[Keep flying and don't look down]

Hummingbirds know
The hand that feeds them
As they hover
With wonder wings

12 beats per second
To an excess of 80

Hummingbirds know
I bring the nectar
A Connecticut Yankee
In San Miguel's court

And I am devout
I am a believer
In wonder wings

And a lover who hovers
As I hover over him

Hummingbirds know
Wonder wings are

The only choice

Diego and Frida

He said: Since art is essential to human life
It can't just belong to the few

She said: I love you more than my own skin

She said: I paint myself so much
Because I am often alone

He wants to go
Without decoration
Naked the way he came in

She wants to go covered
In black lace and scars
A map of her longing

Decorated
The way she became

La Gratitud
[for Collier]

I.

When I'm feeling down these days
And seriously
What's not to be down about?

I remind myself I am
Not that down
About so much else

I love my dearest partner
How we've started late
And made up for lost time

I love our subsequent life
Planting seeds in our garden
Trusting they will grow

And finding lust again
Like back in the day

How we are not young
But we are youthful
And ready to dance

I love him next to me
Reading and listening to music
A simple shared bliss
One must never
Take for granted

He is my beloved
We are a couple
Who knew I could be that
Anymore?
I am so grateful

II.

Mi amor
Somos expatriados
En el paraíso

We know how to take measure
Of a day and of a place

Cómo México
Como este lugar
Es mágico

Y hecho para los amantes

III.

I am here to remind you
In two languages
How faith has been restored
Renovado nuestra fe

No small thing
Considering: Life

And I will continue
To remind you
As you will need to
Remind me

About forgiveness
And patience
And compassion

Como es lo
Que es amor

How that is
What love is

When Color Becomes Suspect

Because this is a weather report
And it's is a Red Alert
With deep fog rolling in

And because it's scary
Driving through it

But not scary like a hurricane
Or a tornado
But scary like a dreary
Shop worn seductress

Who is hated and desired

And driving through this fog
I get the feeling

I get the feeling
That nobody's home
And everybody's home

And walls like blocked arteries
Carry blood away from the heart
And harden all around us

And then color fades away
And we all start to live where it's gray

Because this thing that seduces
Is flat black and white
Stripes on a uniform

And even though that gray
Travels incognito sometimes
If you look closely you will see

Because it's all right there bending
And shaping to fit all things
Right there in front of us
Pretenders on a reality show
All hair-sprayed with laminated smiles

We know them
And we want to be them
Because we know they are not lost
We know where to find them
At 8:00 or 10:00 whenever

And we can agree right here, can't we
They will become our universe

Because this other deal the real deal
We're all so busy pretending
Is not happening
Is a bunch or soldiers sitting in bunkers
Playing cards knowing

There's no need to sweat

Because we're all enlisting one by one
Lining up for duty, our duty
To pursue that gray slate
With no words written on it

And the ones left
The ones with minds like rubber bands
The ones who could cut right through the fog
And show us the way home

We lock them out because we cannot
Pay attention any more
It's all so distracting and hard to think

And we're just not sure
How to feel anymore

So the ones with minds that stretch and snap
And hearts that expand and deflate
Have to be rewound tight
Or run out of town

Because if you question if you challenge
If you insist the world is not worth living in
Without color

If you refuse to forget what it feels like
To lay back and spread your wings
With abandon

What it feels like to hold on tight
How it feels how it feels to let go

If you welcome and even shelter
The strangers, who are you
And you are them
If you open your arms too wide
And leave that soft part exposed

You might be left alone dreaming
Of colors dripping and slipping through fingers
Touching them and tasting them with your tongue
Dancing from yellow to orange to red

And you could decide to stay here
Where the fog has doors and windows

Here, where it is not gray
And it is not easy

But you are never without

Requiem

The edge of the universe
Was slipping away
The Innocents crowded to one side

Their feet trampled
The last patch of soil
Deep and rich beneath them

Soon they would be feasting
On each other, given no other place
To go, and nothing in front of them
But the Hordes

And the Hordes were a sight to see
Grasping at straws, drowning children
Like kittens, milking each others
Bones dry

And the blame! The blame that
Shrunk their bitter hearts
Stoked their rage

And fed their desperately hungry lives
A fat-free, endless refill
Of waste

The Innocents got hip to the real deal:
What's the point of being a martyr
In a land without monuments
To anything but soldiers?

The Innocents had had enough
Of soldering, fighting the Hordes wars
Over greed - but when they tried
To rise up, the Hordes stopped
All story-telling and picture-telling

And anything truth-telling
That moved folks to dance
Or shout - or blow
The Hordes' brains out

The same old new order
Filled the land
The law of the land became
The National Motto:
What works is what sells

The Hordes surrendered
To the screens that became
Their trusted allies
They even stopped hanging out
With each other when they discovered

That they were all the same person
And they hated that person

The Hordes were bored
They bored into hillsides and built moats
Around their fragile castles

But lo and behold
They still had to drink from the water
That surrounded their contaminated land

And the poison filled their blood
And their children's blood
And killed them slowly, slowly
Just like the Innocents

And you had to laugh at their arrogance
Thinking you can't touch this

But by then they were all touched
All that was left to do was stay
In bed and pull the covers
Over their heads

Or become media whores
And reveal all
To the point of distraction

And soon all had been revealed by all
And soon all had been revealed to all

And the gods of necessary illusion
Turned their overburdened backs
On the Hordes

Who had so willfully abused
All their many expensive gifts

The remains of the universe
Fell away
The rich, deep soil nothing
But ashes and dust

And so the Hordes

Taking the Innocents with them

Died unhappily ever after

Unhappily ever after all

Amen

Grounds

Look, the evidence is in
And it's not good
The defense has nothing
To declare

The thing is, how you choose to spend
The rest of your very limited time
And when you think of it that way
Brevity serves a purpose

See, there's no time for details
No time to leave a trail

No time for the tall tales
Of our lives

And I say enough
About safe sex
What about safe head?
What about safe heart?
What about safe
The last dance for me?

Look, I need to know
I need to know
How you want to spend
The rest of your very
Limited time

For you and I, it seems
Brevity serves a purpose
Because the evidence is in

You know it's not good

Part II: Illustrated Poems

Henry Coney Island Miller

In December I go out to Coney Island to see a play adapted from Henry Miller's novel Black Spring. And Henry's there all right, and after the play's over he and I go down to Nathan's, grab us a couple of dogs, and head back up the boardwalk to watch the sun set on a cold Sunday afternoon. And I say to him, 'Henry, your play at Coney Island, it's an inspiration.' And Henry smiles that conspiring smile of his as he leans towards me, his eyes like gleaming picks. 'Baby', he says, 'Coney Island is my middle name.'

This poem includes words from Henry Miller's Black Spring

At the sideshow
by the seashore with
mirrors and magic tricks
and the slick under belly
crooks its juicy finger
You want to eat
fried things
You want to fight
major spasms in your gut.

You want to move into a hiding place for freaks.

Henry Miller is not hiding. He wants to declare he is a traitor among traitors to the human race. And we look, but we cannot bear it. Us whores and faggots and niggers and cunts and kikes. We are all of us equals in the waste and cruelty of our lives.

I go with Henry to his street of early sorrows. Where everything is shoddy, thin as Pasteboard, a Coney Island of the mind. We all come here, finally, and we live in those buildings that cannot hold themselves erect.

He is the bruised red son going down on Coney Island. Henry Miller beats off into the bloody and wild night life. . .

When this mad thing called sleep runs like an eight-day clock, all pain . . . and dull . . . and bearable . . . like this.

Nocterminal

Look, something told me I should just stay in tonight…

But no, I don't pay any attention to myself
I head out on my blades like a lamb to slaughter

And sure enough as soon as I start my laps
around Washington Square this boy, this adolescent type…

Shimmies up on his bike and tries to run me off the road. So I grab
his bike and I won't let go. And now he knows it's him and me

We go down together or not at all. And he's scared and I'm glad
and I won't let go. But when I do I give him a shove...

And he takes a dive, and I call him the expletive deleted he is.
And his friend says, "You hear what she called you?"

And they both start after me. So I cross the park shaking bad

Decide to skip the skate altogether, head for home with a vengeance

Deadbolt the door behind me, and look down from my window

At the smooth dark street below

Mitzi Mitten Who Came
Into My Life and Shined

She had long long legs, Mitzi Mitten, and short white hair.
She was the closest thing to a real live Barbie doll
I had ever seen, I was seven and in love.
She came to visit, but instead of her husband Bob
she brought her lover Bill, we didn't care, we—
the whole family—were in love, she could do
anything she wanted, and we'd hold open her doors
sweep her path and carry her bags.

She and her lover Bill took us girls to Honey Island.
From there, we could see the islands called
Three Sisters, like us.
We fished and rocked in the hammock and brought shells
to lay at the feet of Mitzi Mitten, the feet
at the end of those long long legs.
She explained to us girls the real deal about
cosmetic application, and the exact right way
to apply perfume, which is not by the way
to dab it on your skin, but to spray the air
in front of you, and waltz through the mist just so.

She didn't have any of her own kids, Mitzi Mitten
but she did have Snoop and Smooch, her two stuffed
dog children, who traveled with her everywhere
and were all dressed up with watches that ticked
suspiciously like our own.
She confided to me that they both drank too much
Vodka when she wasn't looking, and that Snoop had
his eye on me when Smooch wasn't looking, but then
they were pretty advanced for their age.

When Mitzi Mitten came to school with Snoop
my big sister was red-faced, but not me.
I knew all the kids were wondering how I got
to be so lucky as to know a real live movie star.
She told my teacher she was thinking about
enrolling Snoop in my school, and could she
ask some questions, please?
My teacher looked at me with raised eyebrows
but I didn't care, I was in love and learning
important things about what it meant
to be a grown up woman, with a mind of her own.

After

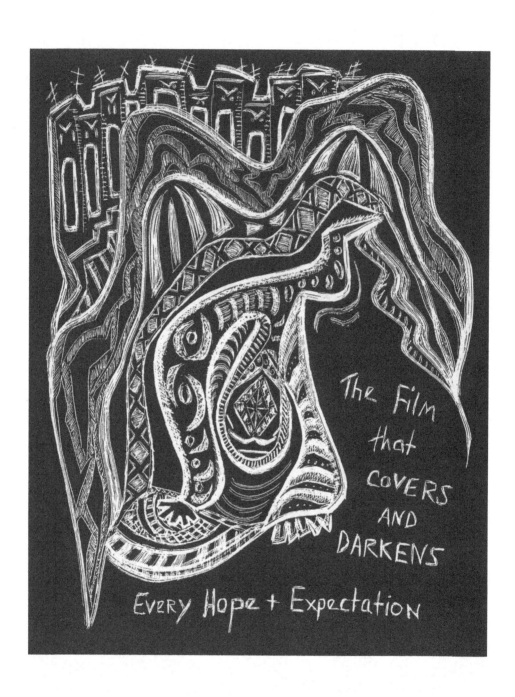

The film that plays in all OUR MINDS—
starring Me, Babe, center stage

After
A TIME HERE
YOU
KNOW
there Never is enough tiME

103

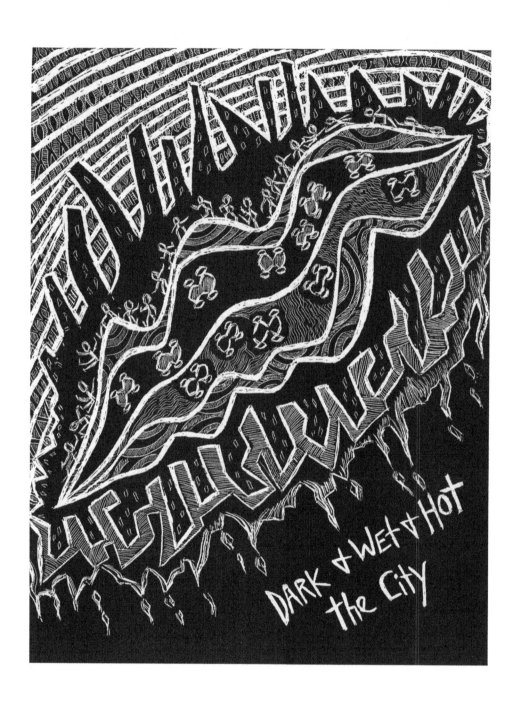

Charged with what remains
when disappointment & Lust
collide

Listen You Man

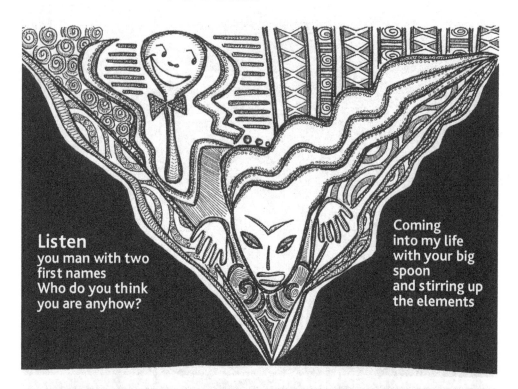

Listen
you man with two
first names
Who do you think
you are anyhow?

Coming
into my life
with your big
spoon
and stirring up
the elements

Bringing up hope from the bottom of the stew
Making the stew taste like caviar

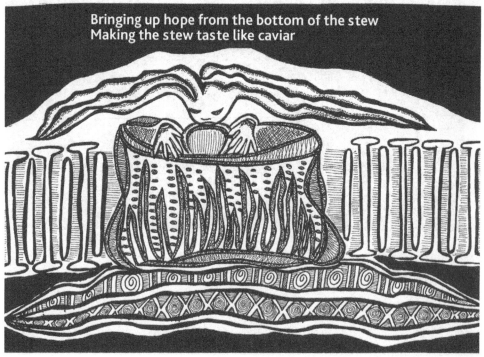

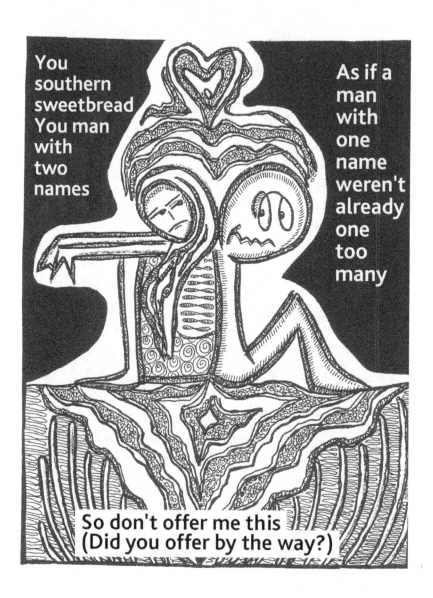

I want
to
forget
you

(I want
to
memo-
rize
you)

I want
to stop
wanting

You
know
I just
want

(to stop
wanting)

Please stop stirring me
just long enough to
Listen

Face of Old Glory

AND
SMILING
A GREEDY
SMILE, with
fiery MANE
SURROUNDING,
EYES LUMINOUS
AND BULGY —
YOU CHOMP AND
GNAW AND SPIT OUT
THE REMAINS,
BELCH AND LAY
BACKWARDS

YOU CLOSE YOUR EYES AND DREAM OF the NEXT MEAL— OF juicy LIPS AND SCALY TONGUE... AND THE DINERS AT YOUR TABLE RAISE THEIR GLASSES to SALUTE YOU

SCHILKE

When Color Becomes Suspect

BUT SCARY LIKE A DREARY
SHOPWORN SEDUCTRESS

who is
hated
AND
DESIRED
AND

DRIVING
through
this
Fog

I GET THE FEELING...

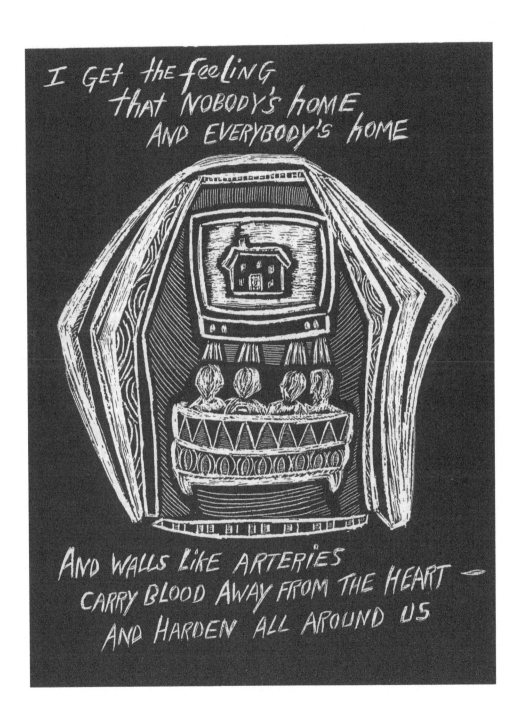

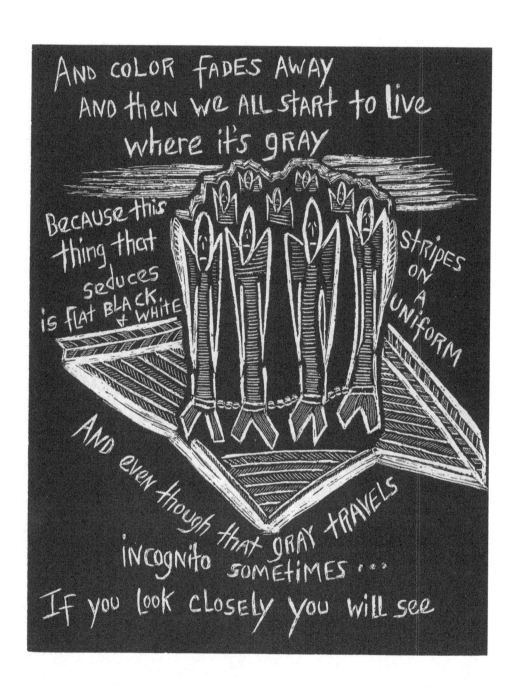

AND COLOR FADES AWAY
AND then we ALL start to live
where it's gray

Because this
thing that
seduces
is FLAT BLACK
& WHITE

stripes
ON
A
uniform

AND even though that gray travels
incognito sometimes...
If you look closely you will see

BECAUSE it's ALL RiGHT tHERE
CHOKiNG AND BENDiNG to Fit ALL tHiNGS
RiGHt tHERE iN FRONT OF US —

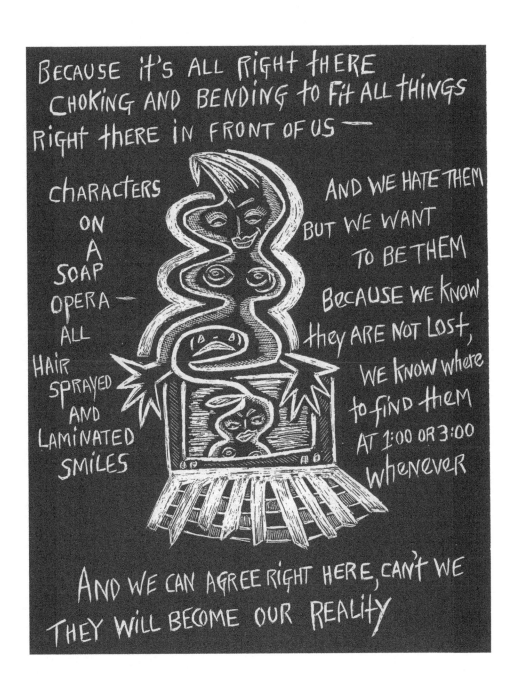

characters
ON
A
SOAP
OPERA —
ALL
HAiR
SPRAYED
AND
LAMiNATED
SMiLES

AND WE HATE THEM
BUT WE WANT
TO BE THEM
BECAUSE WE KNOW
they ARE NOT LOST,
WE KNOW where
to find them
AT 1:00 OR 3:00
whenever

AND WE CAN AGREE RiGHT HERE, CAN'T WE
THEY WiLL BECOME OUR REALiTY

AND the ONES LEFT
the ONES with MINDS
LIKE RUBBER
BANDS,
THE ONES WHO
COULD CUT
RIGHT through
the Fog AND
SHOW US
the WAY home

WE LOCK them out
because we cannot
pay attention
ANYMORE
It's ALL SO
distracting
AND hard to think

AND WE'RE NOT SURE
HOW TO FEEL ANYMORE

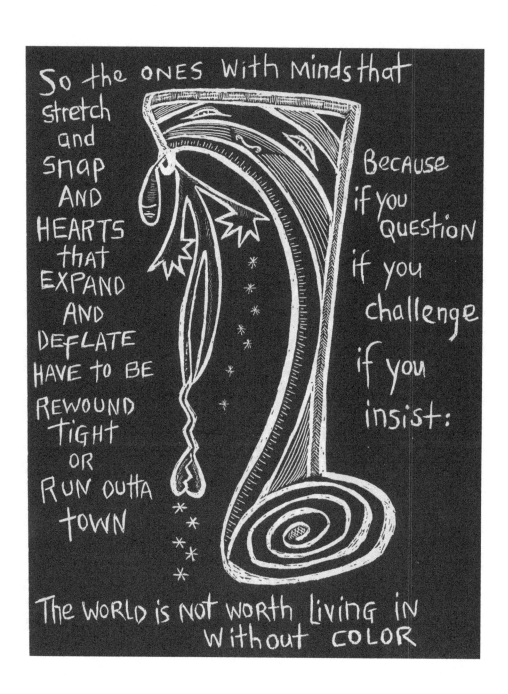

So the ONES With minds that
stretch
and
snap
AND
HEARTS
that
EXPAND
AND
DEFLATE
HAVE TO BE
REWOUND
TiGHT
OR
RUN OUTta
TOWN

Because
if you
QUESTION
if you
challenge
if you
insist:

The WORLD is NOT WORTH LiViNG iN
WithOut COLOR

If you Refuse
to forget what
it feels like
to Lay back
And spread
Your wings
with
Abandon

what it
feels like
to hold on
tight

How it feels
How it feels
How it feels
to Let Go

YOU WILL MOSTLY BE LEFT ALONE DREAMING OF COLORS DRIPPING AND SLIPPING THROUGH FINGERS touching them AND tasting them with your tongue DANCING FROM YELLOW to ORANGE to RED...

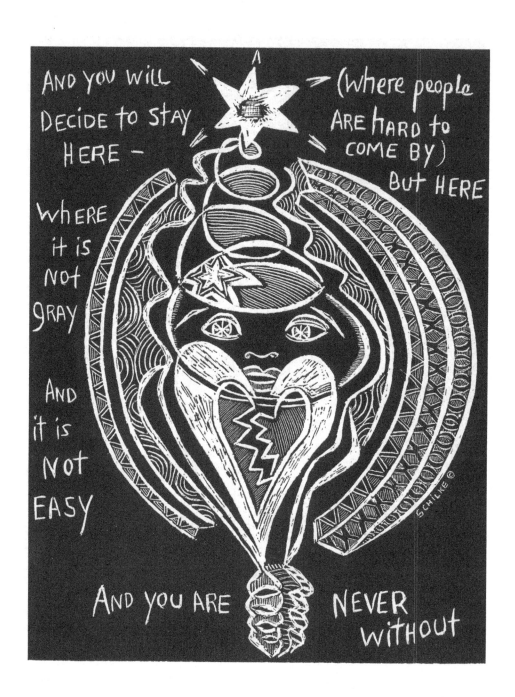

About the Author

 Gaia Schilke is a poet and visual artist who has lived in San Miguel de Allende, Mexico since 2016, and for 3 years before that in Costa Rica. Gaia grew up in Connecticut, lived in Manhattan for 20 years, and then Rhode Island for 10 years before becoming a dedicated expat.

A spoken word poet in NYC, Gaia's poetry and illustrations have been published in numerous literary magazines, journals and books internationally. Her book of illustrated poems & stories, *From the Margin* (Stray Dog Press) was published in 1997. Gaia was the curator of reading series at The Knitting Factory and The Nuyorican Poets Cafe in NYC, and co-creator of the multicultural arts magazine *A Gathering of the Tribes*.

Gaia's book title, *A Coney Island State of Mind*, is in homage to both Henry Miller and to Lawrence Ferlinghetti, whose first poetry collection borrowed a line from Miller's novel *Black Spring* for its own title.

THE WEIRDWOMAN LAUGHS

ALONE
to
herself

AN ECHO
without
REPLY

A
STRANGER'S
BLESSING

SCHILLG

Made in the USA
Monee, IL
27 November 2020